Thomas Miller

Over five seas and oceans

From New York to Bangkok, Siam, and return some reminiscences

Thomas Miller

Over five seas and oceans
From New York to Bangkok, Siam, and return some reminiscences

ISBN/EAN: 9783742891358

Manufactured in Europe, USA, Canada, Australia, Japa

Cover: Foto ©Andreas Hilbeck / pixelio.de

Manufactured and distributed by brebook publishing software (www.brebook.com)

Thomas Miller

Over five seas and oceans

FROM

NEW YORK

TO

BANGKOK, SIAM,

AND RETURN.

———————

SOME REMINISCENCES

BY

THOMAS MILLER.

———————

NEW YORK:
ALBERT METZ & Co., 22 Platt St.

1894.

DEDICATED TO HIS FRIENDS

IN THE

NEW YORK LIFE INSURANCE COMPANY.

PREFACE.

This little story of a few years residence and travel in the East has been written at the solicitation of the author's friends. It makes no claim to great literary distinction, nor does it aspire to rank among the *chefs d'œuvres* of the world of books. It is the plain, unvarnished story of the experiences of a Yankee in the Orient, who presents the illustrations and the printed matter from memory, after a lapse of twenty-seven years, which he trusts is a sufficient apology for all errors.

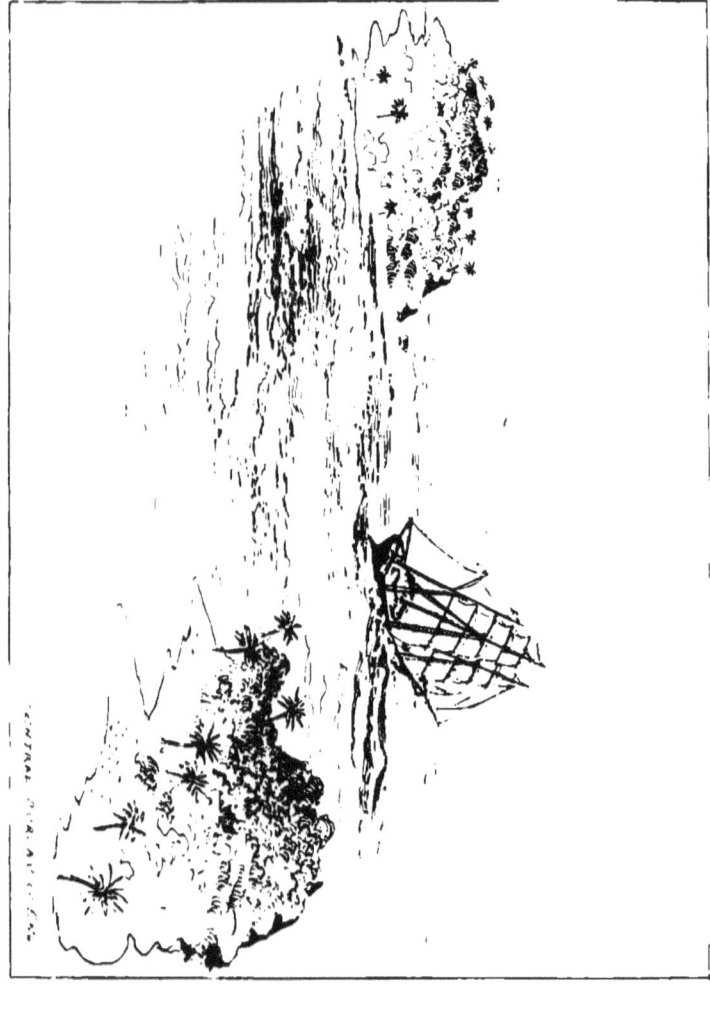

ISLANDS OF AMSTERDAM AND ST. PAUL, INDIAN OCEAN. (Page 7.)

CHAPTER I.

I, WITH three others, sailed from New York on the 4th day of August, 1857, on board of the British barque "Oak," of Hartlepool. We crossed the bar the next day with little or no wind, and laid our course S.E. by E. from the Highland Lights, losing sight of the Lights at dark that night. Our voyage was very pleasant until we crossed the line—the Equator; there, for two or three days, it was rather squally, but not enough to reef topsails. We had a good run until we made the Islands of Amsterdam and St. Paul, two lonely islands in the middle of the Indian Ocean. The next land we made was the Islands of Java and Sumatra about the 20th of November. Arrived at Anjiers in the Straits of Sunda about dark the

same day, after a passage of about one hundred and seven days from New York.

Here we recruited ship with fresh provisions, such as yams, onions, sweet potatoes and fowls. On the third day we weighed anchor, and sailed out into the Straits, with the wind from S.S.W. blowing up the Straits. We passed the Two Brothers Island out in the China Sea. The first Sunday, after we entered the China Sea, at daylight, we were confronted with seventeen waterspouts of huge size, some of which were over two miles off. At one time it looked as if we would be engulfed by them, for certainly, if one of them had burst on us, our good ship would have gone down. A water-spout is a long column of water, rising out of the sea. It begins with a little ripple on the water like a whirlwind, increasing in diameter until ten or twelve feet in size; it then rises, up and up, until it reaches the clouds. It ascends with a corkscrew motion. The only way to get clear of it is to fire a cannon into it,

THE WATER SPOUTS IN THE CHINA SEA.

(Page 8.)

Sometimes the concussion will break the column, and it falls with a terrible noise and splash into the sea. As luck would have it, we had no guns to fire into the worst one; therefore, only by an overruling Providence and a little main strength and smartness in hauling our braces, did our good ship sail clear of the nearest one, which was very large. As it passed us, or we passed it, the noise was almost deafening. Notwithstanding our scare, the sight was perfectly grand. As it was the Northeast Monsoon, we kept well to the southward and eastward up along the coast of Borneo, commonly called the Palawan Passage. We passed large numbers of beautiful islands, until we made nearly a fair wind of it, and sailed direct for the entrance to the Gulf of Siam. We came to anchor off the bar about the 24th of December; took pilot, and crossed the bar and drifted up to Bangkok.

The river is so very crooked we could not sail up; therefore, we drifted up with the tide, and came to anchor in mid stream on the 27th of December, after a passage of one hundred and forty days. The whole distance of about seventeen thousand miles could have been made in a ship's boat.

We were very kindly received by our consignee and the natives. The first native of note I met was the Prime Minister of the Kingdom, who was very friendly. After the machinery was all landed and housed in the godown of the consignee, I was sent to the province of La Consachee to finish erecting a small steam sugar mill. La Consachee is northwest from Bangkok; distance from Bangkok about seventy-five miles. I went in a covered boat, with four stalwart oarsmen and a cook, who acted as interpreter. We journeyed at night and tied up to trees in the daytime. Went ashore to get fruit and to chase monkeys, with which the country abounds. We arrived at our destination in the middle of the third night after leaving Bangkok. Next morning the Governor of the Province called on me, and presented me with what is called a drinking cocoanut, which was very cool and refreshing. It is a fruit filled with natural milk, and very sweet. This fruit is a token of friendship. I lived on the very best provisions the country afforded during my three weeks stay with them. I started up the mill and showed the natives how to run it. The day before I began grinding cane, I requested the Superintendent of the mill to give me as large a pile of cane as he gave the bull mills. He laughed at the idea of my little mill of 12½ x 35 roller grinding as much as the three bull mills. About six P. M. we all started up, and I had to jump around to show the natives how to handle cane; and they handled it so that by 2 A. M. next morning my pile of cane was all used up, and I helped the others to get finished by daybreak, which is about 4.30 the year round. Then there was great rejoicing over the first steam sugar mill erected in Siam. We did not grind again for three nights for the want of cane, so I had a good time going round looking at the country, and seeing how they cut cane. I ran the mill a week, until the natives could handle it, which they did, the third night, without my assistance. They are a very smart, observing people. I left La Consachee for Bangkok, after a trip down stream of two nights and one day.

On landing, I found one of our young men, A. Sharpp, crazy. The doctor called it delirium tremens, but I thought it was sunstroke. He being a British subject, we turned him over to the Consul, after we were worn out watching day and night with him for three weeks. The Consul sent him to Singapore to the hospital, and he died on the passage, and was buried at sea. The captain never handed his effects to the authorities at Singapore, including a twenty dollar gold piece I put in his trunk to buy some little comforts that the hospital did not supply. Sharpp's death left in the gang two engineers and one carpenter,

The carpenter, Mr. Hatch, got some kind of skin disease, which compelled him to leave for home. Then there were only two left, myself and Jenkins. Poor Jenkins turned out badly, and left me inside of two years; thus I was the only one left at Bangkok.

My next move was with my mate to put a pair of 20 x 24 yacht engines in the Prime Minister's yacht, "Meteor." I ran the yacht for some time, until the natives were properly schooled.

The next job was to put in a small single engine for Som Decht Noi's yacht, used for merely a plaything round the river and canals. Som Decht Noi was a very high noble. His title was conferred on him for meritorious conduct. He was a very old man, and was heavy, say about 250 pounds. He wanted me to erect the engine in a saw shed, which I did. He came in the day I started it, and became very much interested and excited at seeing the engine run. He said it was wonderful. As he was leaving the shed, his half-idiotic son took hold of the little flywheel, and it threw him over on a pile of sawed lumber. He had tried the trick several times before, and I had stopped him; but this time, as his father was there, he put on airs, and took hold of the wheel, and got what I had told him. This accident and the excitement of seeing the machinery running, brought on an attack of heart trouble with the old gentleman, and he fell dead on entering his palace. His body was kept one year, and then the funeral pile was built, and the body placed on the top, incased in a gold box or urn. Ten Buddhist priests stood in a row, having in their hands a heavy web of silk. It passed from the last one to the ground. On inquiring, I found that the sins of the man were passing from the body during the incantations of the priests, which never ceased until the pile was all ready for the torch to be applied by the King. This took three days and nights, during which there were theatres, juggling, all kinds of shows with fruits and candies—a three days go-as-you-please.

On the evening before the burning, the King and his nobles were present, and I, with several other foreigners, went up to see the grand display. The King saw me, and sent his page for me. We all sat on mats, with the Prime Minister, Lord Mayor and several others. We laughed and talked until 12 o'clock; then we made our salaam and left. Next day we attended the burning, and, as the custom is, the King scattered limes (a small lemon), in which is money, from one Fuang to Siluing, to a Tical, and some had gold rings. The King saw me and called me, "Ma Millee," to come up to him in the midst of his nobles on a temporary platform. The nobles were on their knees and elbows, while I stood up, and the King filled my pockets with the limes, for which I said, "Cop chie" (thank you), and left. What he gave me contained two gold Fuangs, the rest silver. During all this time the body was burning. When the whole pile was consumed we went home.

The next job was to put up a steam saw mill to saw teak wood. This was a failure on account of opposition from the Chinese sawyers.

Next was a job to put in an engine in the steamer "Jack Waters" for C. A. Allen, of Andover, Mass.; A. J. Westervelt, of New York, and Russell & Co., of Hong Kong. Mr. Westervelt was the shipbuilder and I was the engineer. I put the engine and boiler in the boat before she was decked, and was ready for steam when the boat was launched, except shipping the wheel, which was done, and we went on a trial trip the third day after the boat was put in the water, and it was successful in every particular. The boat was put to towing on the river, which was not a success until the company built some lighters of their own, which they did; then business was flourishing, and kept so for about a year, when Mr. Westervelt became timid and sold his interest

STEAMER "JACK WATERS." (Page 16.)

to me, with the understanding that I was to have
charge of the floating stock, which consisted of
one steamer and three lighters, with carrying capacity of 4,000 piculs, or about 250 gross tons.
Work was fair. Messrs. Russell & Co. sold their
interest, through Chang Lai Soon, an educated
Chinaman, to Williams, Anthon & Co., who assumed the shore work. This went along for a time,
until one Sunday they took it into their heads to
go on an excursion down to the bar. This was
in violation of my agreement, which was that the
boat should not be run on Sunday, no matter
what inducements offered, as my men worked
hard six days and six nights, when called upon.
But my partners took the boat down the river,
Mr. Allen and my native assistant acting as captain and engineer. This act dermined my future
action. Next morning, Monday, I called at Williams, Anthon's & Co.'s office, and stated my ultimatum; namely, I was ready to buy or sell, feeling satisfied in my own mind that they were not

able to manage the property, and the interview ended as I expected: C. A. Allen and Thomas Miller bought out the entire concern. To pay my interest, I borrowed $3,000 from the King's brother, Prince Crom Alouing Wangsau, without interest. We did well for over eighteen months; then business came to a stand still, owing to the heavy crops of rice in China and elsewhere. We did not earn $5,000 in four months. At the same time we were under heavy expense, with about ninety men in our employ. This was very discouraging to us. We agreed to buy or sell by comparing notes. Of course, whichever offered the most took the whole. Mr. Allen offered $1,000 more than I did, and became the sole owner of the steamer "Jack Waters" and four freight barges, and a schooner of about 100 tons.

CHAPTER II.

Y intention was to sail for home, after I came back from my trip to Ayuthia, Prabat, etc., and the interior of the country on excursion.

On or about the 12th of January, 1861, I, with two others, foreigners, started for the trip, after receiving a general letter from the King to the Governors of the several Provinces through which we might pass. This letter ordered that boats, elephants, and all other supplies should be provided for us, which made our journey very pleasant. We started from Bangkok about 6 P. M., and arrived at Ayuthia the next evening about sundown. We called on the Governor by invitation. He met us in his audience hall, with no furniture, except very handsome mats on the floor. He received the King's letter on a silver waiter, read it, and then passed it to his Cabinet to read, and then passed it back to me. Then he asked our pleasure. I told him we wanted seven elephants with howdahs, to carry us and our servants to Prabat and back, a journey of about twelve days, and we wanted breakfast early next morning, so as to get off early in the cool of the day. Next morning we started at six A. M., and made good time crossing rivers and traveling through the jungle. At night fall we came to an old dilapidated temple, where we put up for the night. Our cook prepared our rice, curry, fish and a bowl of tea, after which we laid down under our mosquito nets on our mats, and slept soundly till daybreak. I got the cook up, and he got our rice, curry and fish, with the bowl of tea. After we had breakfast, we started again, and we came out onto a beautiful road with a number of fountains of spring water, where the caravans stopped to water their cattle. There we met a large num-

THE SEVEN ELEPHANTS.

(Page 20.)

ber of pilgrims on their way to Prabat to worship, as this was the season for all devotees of Buddha to assemble on the mountains of Prabat round the footprint of their god. These crowds of people, with their elephants and ox carts, on their way to the shrine of worship, reminded me of the Children of Israel going up to Jerusalem in the days of old to worship.

We arrived at Prabat early in the evening, and presented the King's letter to the Governor of that Province, who received us very graciously, and provided quarters for us. Our cook prepared supper of boiled chicken, rice and curry. We slept very soundly that night. Next morning, after breakfast, we started up the mountain via steps cut zig-zag up its face. It was about 1,000 feet to the top. We met scores of pilgrims coming down. When we got to the top, we entered a very large, beautiful temple, built to cover over what Siamese say is the footprint of Buddha, which was made in the rock when he made his ascent to Heaven; and the natives believe it; therefore, they erected this magnificent temple. It has four walls about 40 feet high, and covering a space of say 75 feet square. The roof is carried without columns or supports of any kind, and the spire goes up to a needle point. On entering this gorgeous temple, the High Priest or Pope of the Kingdom saw us. He sent his page over to where we stood, and he made his salaam to us, and said His Grace wanted to see me, as we had met before in Bangkok. When we drew near, he came down from his throne, and bid us welcome, and conducted us to the footprint, which was about 6 feet long, 2 feet wide and about 4 feet deep, and all covered with gold cloth resting on four columns, overlaid with gold. His Grace caused the worshippers to leave so that we could examine it, which we did, and I found about 15 inches deep of gold leaf. This leaf is put in the cavity or print as an offering which these people make to their gods or idols. This

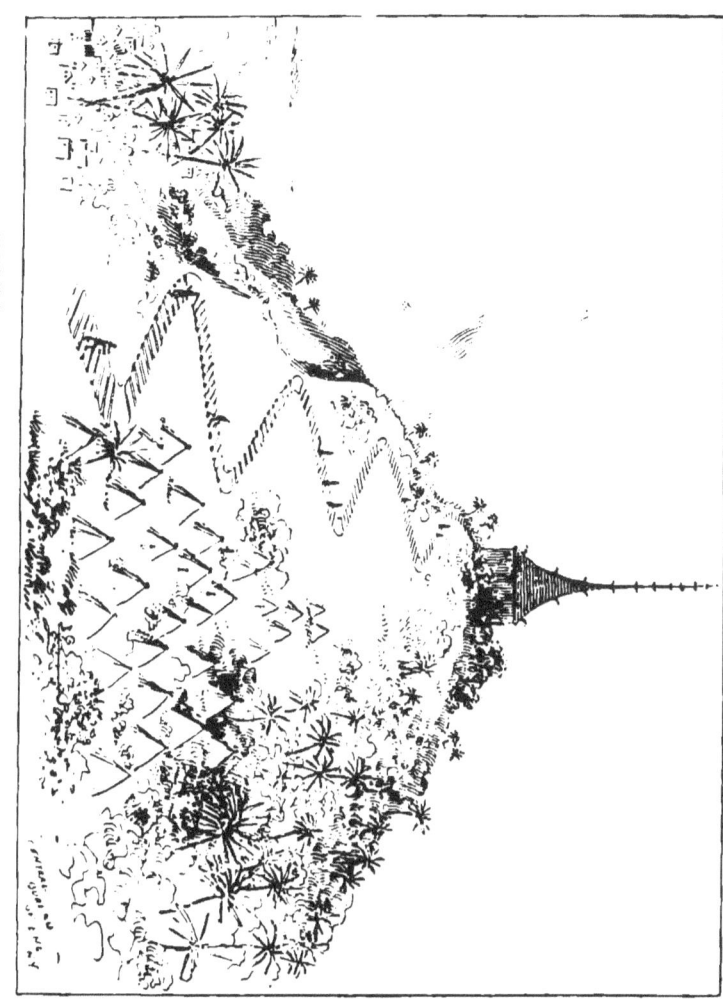

TEMPLE ON THE MOUNTAIN OF PRABAT. (Page 22.)

temple has several idols in it, some of which are very costly. We stayed upon the mountain until long after noon. The natives from all parts of the Kingdom come to Prabat every February to worship. As there are no hotels to live in, they use tents, umbrella shape, and so large that six or eight can sleep under one. They do their cooking outside. The sight to us heathen of the Western Nations was very unique. Only think of looking at thousands of people who go to Prabat to worship as Ancient Israel went up to Jerusalem to worship! After thanking the High Priest for his kindness, we took our leave, and went down and mingled with the worshippers at the foot of the mountain. We found bazaars, market places where everything in the line of vegetables and fish, together with trinkets, some of which were very beautiful, were sold; the trinkets of ivory, brass and filigree silver work; also, Chinese theatres, juggling, snake charming, etc.

On the second day after our arrival at Prabat we started in a westerly direction toward Nocburrie, over the beautiful road through the jungle. We passed an old temple built by the road side, in the shape of an old fashioned Quaker meeting-house, with a belfry on top, out of which grew a tree, say about sixty feet high, known out there as the Bude Tree. We call it in our country Sycamore, with heavy foliage. The roots ran down the belfry to the roof, down the roof, and so on down to the ground, from which it took its nourishment. It was a grand sight. We arrived at Nocburrie Saturday evening. The Governor placed us in an ante-chamber which was half way decent. Our grub was very fair. We lay up all Sunday, and Monday started again on our voyage of discovery. We opened up into a most beautiful level place, covered with grass and shrubbery. Our guide gave us an elephant race, and it was a race very exciting, and full of pain and soreness next day. We

TEMPLE IN THE JUNGLE. (Page 24.)

stopped at a temple over night and dined on cold rice and sugar, as our supplies were nearly out. Our breakfast consisted of sugar and rice. We started about noon, and we came to a Laos village, where we got a supply of rice, fish and palm sugar, which is very good, also a few fowls. Here let me say that Laos women are, as a general thing, very pretty and very tidy. The village was very neat and clean. With them, as with the Siamese, the women do the work of buying, selling, and doing all their business. We stayed in this village over night, and its surroundings were beautiful. The houses were surrounded by clusters of bamboos, which grew ten or twelve in a cluster and from two to six inches in diameter and from twenty to fifty and seventy-five feet high. Very beautiful. The natives use the bamboo for a thousand and one purposes--from ornaments to rafts to build houses on; thus the floating houses we read about. Strange to asy, if a man does not like his location, he can pull up stakes and drop down with the tide to another location. We made another start, and crossed an immense paddy or rice field. When in the centre of it we could not see the boundaries on either side. We traveled on out to level ground, which was very picturesque, with flowers and other shrubbery; also a large herd of oxen grazing. On this plain we saw rather a singular sight—three stones, almost perfect spheres, on top of one another, the largest in the middle. What held them, I can't say. The bottom stone was about one-third in the ground. It certainly was curious. We passed on till we came to some bamboo houses, where we stopped over night. After breakfast of rice and fish and tea, started on our homeward trip, and arrived at Ayathua about dark. Discharged our guide and elephants and gave money presents to elephant drivers, etc. After bidding the Governor and others good-by, we left for Bangkok in our boat, and arrived there the next afternoon, tired

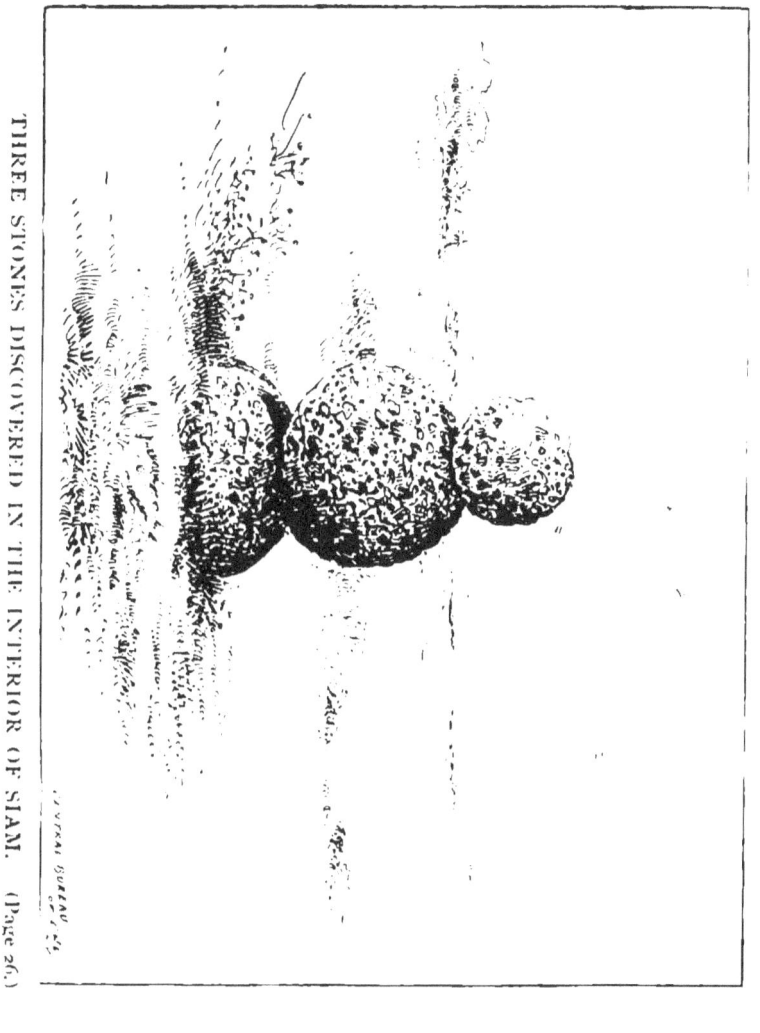

THREE STONES DISCOVERED IN THE INTERIOR OF SIAM. (Page 26.)

out with our journey of about fifteen days, amidst the rejoicing and congratulations of friends, who gave us a grand dinner, such as we did not have during our absence.

I was perfectly well satisfied with the trip. It gave me a store knowledge of the country and of the people; and, I am prepared to say, the Siamese are just the finest people east of the Cape of Good Hope. Just before we left Bangkok on our trip, C. A. Allen bet me a suit of clothes he would be in America and at home before I would. Of course, I being so positive, and had made all arrangements for my passage to Hong Kong in the "Viscount Canning," a large steamer belonging to Pr Pa San, a very rich Chinaman, merchant, which had not yet arrived, but was expected daily. So I rested very quietly, taking things easily, smoking my Manilla No. 2, which I then thought was very fine. Allen came to me on the second day after getting back and said, "Old chap, I want to go home to see my sister and other relatives whom I have not seen in thirteen years, and if you will stay in my place I will give $3,000 per annum and all expenses and $800 for traveling expenses home." I said, "Charley, I will sleep over it." Next morning I accepted his offer. In less than two hours we were in the United States Consulate, and a power of attorney signed, sealed and delivered. On our way up to the office he told me why he wanted to get away. First, he was sorry I took him up in the purchase. Second, as he had borrowed a large amount of money and was afraid the parties would sell him out, and he did not want the disgrace. The truth of the matter just here is, I was sorry I did not get the concern. I knew there was money in it. Allen sailed for Hong Kong; from there to San Francisco, where he got a new suit of American clothes, and was photographed, and sent a picture, written on the back of which was, "You paid for these," which was the first time I had thought of the bet.

Allen had not gone two weeks before work came in, and we were all busy, night and day, for eight months. Made money hand over fist, so that I paid his debts, paid for a whole new set of machinery, paid for 14x20-inch engines and boiler £1,200 or $6,000. Built a dock to haul vessels in for repairs. Built a wharf, blacksmith shop, hospital, carpenter shop, and built a new lighter, 110 feet keel, 20 feet beam, 10 feet depth of hold, to carry 3,500 piculs of rice, 206 tons, and built a coal shed and put in it 300 tons of Swansea coal at $10, $3,000. I did all this in fourteen months, and had in hand about $4,000 when he arrived out again, and for all of which he was well pleased. I omitted to say that I sent him drafts while at home, amounting to about $3,000.

CHAPTER III.

ON the 8th day of February, 1862, Mr. Allen took charge of his business and gave me a splendid dinner, at which were all the Consuls of the different nations. When the cloth was removed, Mr. Allen arose at the table and, after eulogizing me for the way I had acted since 1859 to the present, more especially the last fourteen months, he presented me at the close with a Frodsham gold watch and chain, which cost at Tiffany's, New York, $600. The presentation was unexpected to me. I replied, thanking him for so valuable a gift. Of course, I said I was not worthy of it, as I had only done my duty. Then there were speeches made by all the Consuls. Sir R. Schamburg, in his speech, made mention of a lawsuit between the British Government and the Siamese Government, he for his country and I on the side of the Siamese. He terminated his remarks by saying I beat him; then I went on to tell the company that two unfortunate engineers were hired by Capt. Bush in Singapore to take charge of the engines of the Siamese steamer "Tiger" on her trip from Singapore to Bangkok. The two men went on board to their duty immediately and ordered the Siamese firemen to fire up, when there was little or no water in starboard boilers. The natives told the men of this important fact, and still they did fire up. The consequence was they burned the crown sheets over the fires, thus ruining the boiler for future use until thoroughly repaired. I was called by the Prime Minister to survey the damages, which I did, and reported the boiler unfit for use. The British Consul sent the engineers from an English steamer to make a survey, which they did. The engineers who burned the boilers sued the King for their money, about $60 each, through the Consulate. The King requested me, through the Prime Minister, to take up the Siamese side of the suit. On the day of trial, Her Majesty's Counsel gave me the seat at the right of the clerk. The suit began by first appointing six assessors or jurors. I told the counsel to select all from his own countrymen, which he did. The reports of the English engineers were read, with a long letter on charity, showing that the two engineers were very poor and needed what they sued for. As defendant, I received the report, and the balance of the letter I laid on the table, to be taken up further on in the trial. All the witnesses for the plaintiff were examined, after which Her Majesty's Counsel rose in his seat and decided the case ended in favor of the engineers, and he would give them the full amount of their claim. Everybody was perfectly amazed at such conduct. I arose from my seat and checked him in his bombast. I gave him to understand I was there as defendant's counsel, and demanded of him, as Her Majesty's Counsel, the right to be heard, and asked him where he got the law that authorized him to decide a case ended when there were two sides to be heard. I said it was not the law of any commonwealth or nation. I therefore protested against his action in this case, and would now proceed with our side. I called up first one and then the other of the plaintiffs and, by cross-examination, proved by them that they were intoxicated at the time the burning of the boiler occurred, and that they were told that the boiler was nearly empty of water, and that they did not know what they were doing —and put that in as a plea. The defendant rested and gave Her Majesty's Counsel the liberty to sum up his side of the case, which he declined. So I took our side, and showed by the action of two drunken men, which I proved by their own evidence in cross-examination, and I showed by their acts that they had thrown a pall of discontent and dissatisfaction over American enterprise in Siam. I told Her Majesty's Counsel that by his act that day, had it been carried out, he would have had the Siamese believe the boiler was defective. I said they were as fine a pair of boilers as ever were put on a ship of its size, and that Americans can build boilers and machinery equal to, if not superior to, any other nation. With these few remarks, I would place the case in the hands of the jurors, hoping that they would judge the case by the evidence, and not by any charitable instincts of their good nature, but let me do the charity act. The jury gave us the verdict without leaving their seats, greatly to the discomfiture of Her Majesty's Counsel, amid the cheers of the visitors in the court room—say about 200, natives and foreigners. I took my papers and left the court. The counsel hardly spoke to me when I left. When I got to my boat, ready to go back to my office, I was met by the two engineers, who expressed much regret that I should have gone so hard against them. I explained why I did it. It was to draw out in the trial where the fault lay—whether it was sheer negligence, brought on by drunkenness, or whether the American boilers were defective in their make-up; and I was satisfied that I had upheld the American mechanic, of which I was one. Then I told them to get in my boat and go with me to my office, and I would show them that the King did not wish to wrong them. So I paid each man his demand ($60), and took separate receipts, which made them happy for the time being. Next morning I reported to the Prime Minister the verdict. Of course he had already heard, and met me at his palace door most cordially and thanked me for the interest I took in Siamese matters. I then told him what I had done with the engineers, and he said that was right; for, said he, the money we don't care for—it is the cause of the accident and what is the remedy. Thereupon, he gave me an order on his treasurer for $120. Thus ended the lawsuit. When the steamer "Chow Phyar" arrived from Singapore with the mails, she brought a number of the Singapore "Times," which had an editorial on the Siamese lawsuit in Bangkok, in which the English were beaten by me.

During my residence in Bangkok, I made several trips to Purchaburrie, the King's summer palace, which is built on top of the mountain, a perfectly beautiful spot. From it can be seen the Gulf of Siam and the Plankplaisoi Mountains, and all the surrounding country, which is very beautiful. There are several small temples and caves, which are fitted up with innumerable idols, large and small, from 15 inches to 20 feet high. The largest cave is a natural cavity in the mountain, with small opening going out from it. The natives have cut a winding zigzag stairway leading down to the bottom. This cave is in the woods. From this cave I got by purchase three idols as curios. I was in two or three other caves of less note. I always enjoyed a week or two up in the mountains of Purchaburrie. The river is very winding. On one of my visits the water was low. We got the "Jack Waters" up by handwork and, for fear the boat would get stuck on some of the points in the river, sent her down to the bar, and I followed the fourth day. On my way down in the ship's boat I saw a large herd of monkeys on the beach. There were several that were over two feet high when on all feet, and with great teeth. I thought I would have a little fun with them, so I went on shore. The monkeys ran up the hill. When on top, they held a council of war, chattering and shaking their teeth. One of the largest started for me, the rest followed. The natives yelled to me to "Rhu! Rhu!"—run! run!— which I did with all the speed I could. They told me afterwards that if I had stood my ground I would have been killed, and I believe it. Only think, over a hundred monkeys attacking a man. The natives told me before I started for them not to do it, as they would "Tatlow"— cut me, kill me—and I was glad to get on the boat again. I never troubled a lot of monkeys again. I had one at my office, also a bull terrier dog and an otter, all pets, and they would play together as a happy family. The monkey would sit on bamboo lounge at noon after I had my tiffin, or lunch at one o'clock. He would smooth my hair, and I would go to sleep, wake up and find him lying beside me fast asleep, thus presenting two monkeys asleep. The dog would go down and up the river on the boat, and if the boat left without him, the Chinamen on the lighters would come ashore for him with their sanpan. He would do their fighting for them. The sailors would not come on the lighter without I or the pilot was there. The otter was a perfect pet. He would wiggle up on the piazza, then up on my lap, and kiss me, no matter how clean my clothes were; then get down and play around my feet and squeal, and if I spoke sharply to him, he would go down and get into the river and swim around. He would do anything I told him, such as going off in the river to a fisherman's boat, steal a fish, then come back to the landing and eat it. Thus I passed my leisure hours with my three pets. In dull times I would take a trip to Ayathua, or Blank Plasoi, on the east coast of the gulf, and spend several days every year. It is a fishing village, also a Baptist Mission station. There is a beautiful beach for bathing. I generally took three or four outings every summer—Ayathua, Purchaburrie, Blank Plasoi, etc. The main cause of my success was doing just as I said, whether it pleased or not.

On a certain occasion I called on the Prime Minister, who owed me about $700. It was as good as gold, but this time the British Consul had some drafts for sale on the Royal Treasury of London, and I wanted to buy to send home to my family. So I called on him for what was due. He asked through his Secretary what I wanted, as he was a little off that morning; that was the cause of his sarcastic inquiry and his not meeting me as he always had done, in a more cheerful, friendly way. I told him, through the same channel, my errand; that I wished to send some money home, and that there was a chance for me to buy some drafts, and the mail steamer was to sail that day; therefore, if he would let me have the amount due, he would oblige me. He replied, if I was a gentleman I would not ask him for money. I got my Dutch up, and asked the secretary if he would tell His Excellency what I said. "You will please tell him if he was a countryman of mine and Prime Minister, and say I was no gentleman, because I asked him for my just dues, I would slap his mouth." He laughed, and gave me an order on his treasurer for the money. He was a better friend, if possible, than ever, and told the United States Consul that I was a man in every way.

CHAPTER IV.

WHEN the new engines and boiler for the "Jack Waters" arrived out from Gardner & McIntosh, New Cross, London, and I got my dock ready to dock the boat, the Prime Minister hired me his yacht "Meteor" at $100 per day, and I pay all expenses until I got the "Jack Waters" ready. Of course I did not pay for days she did not run. She averaged four days a week, and I paid him. This leads me to receiving and landing the machinery. I erected a large pair of shears on my wharf for the purpose of lifting heavy boilers and machinery out of vessels for myself and others. The first to use them was the King, who had a consignment of machinery from the Novelty Iron Works, N. Y. In doing the work I hurt my ankle very badly, but did not break the skin. It caused me to lay up for two months without relief. I told Dr. Campbell that if I was a surgeon, I would have known what to do with that leg. He asked me, "What would you do?" I said, "Cut it," which he did with his old saw blade. He made three cuts, and I got ease. Then he put flaxseed poultice on, and I went to sleep, and felt very much better when I got up. During the time my leg was so very sore, my own machinery arrived, and I had to attend to the discharging it from the ship. One day, when standing on the ship's rail, cheering the men at the crab—the boiler was nearly up out of the hold of the vessel—who should appear, walking up the wharf, but my friend Jenkins, dressed with a sailor jacket and hat. I requested him to go up on the piazza and take a seat, and I would follow him when I got the boiler landed, which I did. We shook hands. I enquired after his welfare and of his future. He had no thought for the future, as he had done wrong in leaving his ship in Singapore. He had been chief-engineer on the steamer "Chaw Paar," but drink got him out of it. To encourage him, I told him I would give him work. He asked what to do. "Ah," said I, "at anything I can find for you, and I am ready to give you $125 per month and board. This caused tears to come in his eyes, for he did not expect such kindness, after treating me as he had. I told him that was passed with me, and he must look ahead, so I kept him working until I started for home. Then I put him in first engineer of the "Jack Waters." When I docked the "Waters" for repairs, and put the new machinery in, I made him boss of the job, with Mr. Jackson, my engineer, to help him when he could. I was laid up with my sore leg. When the "Waters" went into dock, I put new garboard planks in, also thoroughly overhauled her by putting new knees and also knee braces ½ inch by 2 inch iron, so as to strengthen her, as she got a powerful twisting by being put on the sunken junks at the mouth of the river by a Portuguese man-of-war brig we were taking out. The tide was running out strong, and the pilot, to clear the junk, shoved the "Waters" on the other junk. We passed out of the river, and the tide was too low to go over the bar. We came to off Mud Point, where we grounded in the mud. Dropped anchor to prevent swinging on the turn of the tide. We lay there two or three hours, until one of the fireman came and told me the boat was making water fast, and I told the pilot to cast off from the brig and make for the mud flats, and put on all steam, and drove the boat high upon the mud, over two miles from the brig. Next morning, about eight o'clock, we floated off. We pumped the water out. Strange to say, the boat did not make any water for six months after —never made a drop, and we had to put water in her to keep her clean. When we took off the garboard plank, we found the mud so thoroughly packed in between the timbers, we had to cut it out with hammer and chisel. This novel way of calking ship with mud just shows what a Yankee can and will do in emergencies. While the boat was in the dock, we put her new machinery in, strengthened her, put new deck on; in fact, made her a new boat. The fact is, the "Waters" was always too light for the work I put her to. I made her do all she could and more. She cut off five crank pins in one month; at another time, broke the top cylinder head in pieces, which we replaced with boiler plate. Another time the boat was coming up the river with $66,000 in treasure consigned to three merchants. I was waiting for her; about 2 A. M. I saw a boat pulling up the river. When near enough I asked Jackson, the engineer, where the "Waters" was. He answered, "Dropping up with the tide." It flashed on me that another crank pin had gone. "Yes," said he, "and the cylinder is broken from one side of the steam chest to the other." About

4 o'clock she got to the wharf, and I got the boxes of treasure on three sanpans, with us three white men, Miller, Jackson and West, one in each, and we delivered the treasure to the con signees. Here let me say, that I doubt very much if I could go from the Battery to Fourteenth street, on the North River, with that amount of treasure in open boats, and not be molested, here in enlightened America or England. After we returned to the boat, I gave orders to take the cylinder off and clear the wreck. After breakfast we turned to repair it. I had no experience with broken cylinders, but, as I have always brought my mind to bear upon emergencies, I made two check rings of brass and fitted them close, and all solid, put the cylinder back, and connected it up and put 75 pounds of steam on. It leaked some. I was prepared for that, and I melted about 100 pounds of lead, made a coffer dam of clay, then poured the lead round the cylinder. When cold, calked it.

which made it perfectly tight. The boat did her work for six months after, and, strange to say, never broke a crank pin. The second day after after we floated her out the dock, we got steam up and I hobbled on board with my cane and the assistance of one of my boatmen. I looked her all over to see that everything was ready. I gave the engines little steam. Jenkins and Jackson down below, seeing all went right, after working slow for some time, I ordered the boat to be cast off, and we went down the river ten miles, everything working fine. On our return I let the engines out to see what they would do. They registered 90 revolutions per minute, which was grand for new engines. I put the "Waters" to work on the third day after coming out of the dock. In the midst of work, one of my Tycoons or captain, named Check Churie, fell and broke his leg. As I had a sick hospital or room on the ground, he was put in this room, and Dr. Campbell called. Here let me say that Dr. Campbell received from each foreigner's house located in Bangkok $200 per annum, whether there was any sickness or not. The doctor set the leg, and put on it the usual appliances. The Tycoon did not like the English doctor's treatment, so, after two weeks of complaining, I got out of patience and told him to get his Chinese doctor, if he wanted to, not wishing to stand in his way of getting well. He sent for his Chinese doctor, who came down and took off Dr. Campbell's appliances, and put his own on, which consisted of what appeared to be a putty made of lime and vermilion red, and, strange to say, that in three weeks the man was walking about the compound with a crutch. Neither Dr. Campbell nor myself could understand how it could be possible for a man with a broken leg to get up and around so soon. The man was at his work in about two months. Any man that got sick or hurt in my employ was paid for his time and fed, and a man to take care of him until he returned to work.

During the time I was laid up with a lame ankle, I bought a large boatload of wood for starting fires on the steamer and other purposes. Wood is sold by 100 pieces, at different prices, according to length and size. I agreed with the boatman to count the pieces and pile the wood up in two ranks or piles, as I could do nothing but growl at everything and everybody. I watched the man pitch the wood ashore, at the same time counting the pieces. He would call out "ing, song, see, hoc, jit, caw, sip"—one, two, four, six, eight, nine, ten. Thus, you see, I was being cheated out of three pieces in every ten. He kept this up until all was on shore; then I called out my interpreter, asked him to count ten. He began, "ing, song, sam, see, ha, hoc, jit, bat, caw, sip." Then I told how the man counted, and ordered him to go and tell the man how he counted the wood, and to count it over and pile it up. He declined, saying his count was correct. I told him if he did not count it over, and give me a correct count, I would have him arrested. This put the quietus on him, and he recounted the wood with my man keeping tally. When done, I was very nearly 500 pieces less than he said at first. The above is only one of the great many tricks they have to cheat foreigners. Of course, they are very honest with good watching; at the same time, I will say that if you make a confidant of any one of them, he will do his duty.

To illustrate: I had in my strong box in the office 5000 ticols and the building was not strong-built of bamboo. I said to the man, "ow henna heep nung, ha pan bat anny"— do you see the box, 5000 ticols in it. This man kept his word, so that I had the money to pay my help next day.

Another instance of their shrewdness: a mate of an English ship I was loading kept tally of a cargo of rice, and cheated me out of 25 bags or picols, and signed the boat note or receipt for 25 bags less than its face. I told the tycoon, or captain, of the lighter. He said he "can do, makee all the samee good next time." So he did. When he went to the ship and discharged his lighter, he was 75 bags ahead. I compelled the mate to sign the boat note 75 bags over. He did not want to do it, but I told him he signed the last 25 less, and of course he must sign this one 75 over. At the same time, I knew there could be none over or none less, from the fact that every bag that goes on board the lighter the tycoon takes the piece of bamboo that is stuck in the bag when it leaves the go-down; therefore the same number must be counted out that was counted in. When I took the boat notes to the merchant it was all right, for he knew all about miscounts as well as I did. Thus I was brought to learn more thoroughly to count in their dialect, as follows, which will be as a key to their language, as I often remarked that a person must of necessity keep his or her mouth full of betel nut to say: "ing,¹ song,² sam,³ see,⁴ ha,⁵ hoc,⁶ jit,⁷ bat,⁸ caw,⁹ sip,¹⁰ sip bet,¹¹ sip song,¹² sip sam,¹³ sip see,¹⁴ sip ha,¹⁵ sip hoc,¹⁶ sip jit,¹⁷ sip bat,¹⁸ sip caw,¹⁹ ye slip.²⁰"

This brings me to another source of my success. A rich Chinaman named Poo Yin, who owned several ships, came to me one Sunday morning, and said his ship, Five Stars, was at the outer anchorage, and he wanted her towed up. I told him it was Sunday, and my men wanted rest, and I always gave them that day until seven o'clock in the evening. Then the boat went down the river. He asked my price. I told him $200. He offered me $400, just double. I said no; not but what I wanted to oblige him, but I could not violate principle for money. At the same time I asked him when he wanted his ship up. He answered by sunrise next morning. I told him he should have her up by that time. He went off satisfied that I would do what I said. I sent the boat down with instructions to lay the lighters alongside of the ships and then take in tow the Five Stars, and bring her up to Bangkok, but if the weather is fine, why wait for them and bring them all up to Packet Canal, let the barges go through and pick them up at the end and take the ship round the big bend. Monday morning about four o'clock, I heard the "Waters" whistle round Petticom's Point. I hustled to get out in my boat to meet them, which I did, the ship and four lighters. I boarded the ship, and she dropped the lighters, as we went up the river to their proper consignees. Then we went up opposite Poo Yims go-down and dropped anchor. I moored ship. I left for home, and got my breakfast, and then went to business, seeing the lighters were getting loaded and their boat notes on board. Then I let them drop down the river so the steamer could pick them up. This done, I returned home to Tiffin or lunch. While performing that pleasant duty, a messenger came in from Poo Yin with four hundred Mexican dollars. My boy counted the money in two sections or piles. One pile I kept; the other I sent back with my compliments. About 4 P. M., Poo Yin called to know why I sent $200 back. I told him inasmuch as I did not send the steamer expressly for his ship, of course, I would only charge my price, $200; but said I, if I held the steamer back for the lighters, of course I would take $400 for I would lose a trip. He went off pleased and and I got all his work from that day forth.

This reminds me of a little matter that might have proved fatal, namely, there was a man, an American, keeping a sailor boarding-house up near San Pang or market place. He was taken sick and died. He made his will, and gave his sister what he had, after paying his debts. During the latter part of his sickness I had to hire a man to take care of him. I hired a man named Redmon from Orleans County, N. Y., who came to us as a sailor, and got sick or left his ship, I can't say which. However, I hired him at $1 per day. As he was not doing anything, he was glad to get it. He was an ugly character, as I found out afterwards. The sick man died a few days after. I told the man Redmon to call and get his money, $16, which he promised to do. In the meantime I heard that the United States Consul held a claim in the Consulate against Redmon for $25 for killing J. S. Parker's dog. I again asked him to call for his money, as I must have a voucher for the money. He answered, "I will," and did not until the Consul garnisheed the money in my hands, which I did not pay over to the Consul, thinking I might get Redmon off from paying the $25. He called for his money, and I told the situation, but told him to go down to the Consul with a letter I wrote him about the matter. Instead of so doing, he went off and got full of arick, or samshoo, that will make one crazy drunk. In this condition he went down to the Consulate, and drove the Consul out of the Consulate, with two single barrel pistols and a large bowie knife, 12 inches long in the blade. When he could do no more, he turned his attention to me. We met on the steamer's landing. He asked for his money. I told him I had done all I could do until the Consul answered my letter which he carried down. I then started up the steps to the piazza. I heard a click; I turned to see what it was. Just then he pulled the trigger the second time, and it missed fire. He threw it away into the wood pile, and pulled another from his pocket, and said, "Damn you! give me my money, or I will kill you." With that, he pulled the third and fourth time, and missed fire. He threw that one in the wood pile. He then drew his bowie knife, and made for me. I then slapped him on the shoulder, and told him he was too big a coward to use his knife against an unarmed man. This excited him more than he was. He repeated the word coward three or four times, then made a cut at me, and broke his knife off at the handle, by striking the rail which I was leaning upon at the time. By this time several men from the next compound came in and took the knife from him. Just then the United States Marshal came onto the scene, and I ordered Redmon's arrest. The Marshal put a pair of handcuffs on him. In less than five minutes he broke them, solid iron. Captain White, of the ship "John W. White," brought a set of chain handcuffs which he could not break. He was put in jail at the Consulate, and made so much noise that the natives ran away. The Consul sent for me to take him away. Not I, but I cooled his fighting propensity by going into the jail. There he was, as wild as a madman. He saluted me by asking, "What do you want?" I told him I was prepared to quiet him. I said, "You came at me with pistols and bowie knife yesterday, and I did not have a jack knife." I measured across the room, went out and had the natives make me a pair of stocks for his feet. When done, I took them in, and made him put his feet in the holes, and I screwed them up. I did not have any weapon. He was kept that way until he got the whisky all out of him, and he got all right. Then they were taken off. He was indicted for attempting my life. He pleaded guilty. He was asked if any one would defend him. After he was condemned, before sentence, I pleaded for him. He looked so penitent. I got him off with ten years in Sing Sing, and he was sent to Hong Kong in double irons, and from there he was sent to the United States in a man-of-war. As luck would have it, the papers sent by the Consul were not sufficient to hold him, therefore he was let go. I gave him pipes and tobacco to last him up the sea to China. The next I heard of him he was in Singapore, sick in the hospital with derangement of the liver. I sent him some money, as I believed he would never have done what he did if sober.

CHAPTER V.

HERE are many little items I could refer to with pleasure, such as dinners and buryings, etc. I will mention one or two.

First: I had some business with Krom Aloing Wang Saw, the King's brother, a large, heavy man, about 300. I called with my boat on him. On entering the palace grounds, I met the King and his children coming out of the palace, where he had been to the top-knot cutting of the Prince's eldest son. What I mean by cutting the top-knot is this: Male children's hair is allowed to grow on the top of the head from birth until they mature. Then it is cut. With royalty it is a great feast, with royalty and nobles assembled to do honor to the young man.

I passed the King, who bowed with his military cap lifted very graciously. I stood and saluted him. I started on to the palace, and just as I got to the inner gate, who should face me but the Queen, with a large number of Amazons or female soldiers. They looked neat and tidy. In the rear was a young corporal. She looked at me and laughed. I said to the corporal, "Will you take me in your army?" She laughed aloud, and set the rest at it. The Queen looked back to see the cause of the merriment. Of course I stood as quiet as a lamb, with my face serene. I told the old Prince what I passed through. He laughed, and put his big fat arms around me and said I was a good American. I got through with my business, and left him with the usual salaam.

This brings me to a little affair I had with the second King. The second King could talk good English. He was taught by Mr. Jones and other American missionaries. The King built himself a very nice steam yacht, and put the engines in the boat. He did very well, except some little things. He sent his royal barge with 60 paddlers for me. Of course I went up to his palace, which is very beautiful, neat and trim, with beautiful gardens. He met us at the King's landing. At first the sentry on the landing would not permit me to land on the King's landing, but I insisted on doing so. Finally, the King came in sight, and he told the sentry to let the barge come into the landing. We met, and we had some refreshments, such as drinking cocoanuts, coffee and cakes. We talked awhile, telling me many things about the country and himself. His heir apparent was named Prince George, after our own George Washington, as he was always a great admirer of Washington. We went on board of the boat. I packed, and showed his men how to pack the engines, and wanted to know where he should put the clock, meaning the steam gauge and the whistle. I set a drill and set his men drilling a hole in the steam drum, and when done, I tapped the hole. In doing so I wanted a screw wrench, and said to one of the men "Kon kie me." The King said, "Hold on, what did you ask for?" I answered, "Kon kie me." "Well," said he, "you are a better Siamese than I am" He persisted in calling it kon, which means hammer. Kie means something to turn a screw with. So I put the two together, and called it kon kie. The King gave in I was right. I put the gauge and whistle up. We got up a little steam, and turned the engines over at the wharf, and I blew the whistle, which pleased him very much, and the gauge he watched with interest. First I had to explain how the steam turned the screw round to the figures. I told him he could carry 70 or 80 pounds, if he wanted to. He thanked me for the service I rendered him. I saw him many times on the river with his yacht.

Another rather laughable affair took place. The Prime Minister, Cala Holme, called at my place of business. When he arrived I was at dinner. As it is the custom of the country never to disturb or be disturbed while eating, he took a seat. The mail steamer "Chow Phyar" arrived that afternoon, and the captain sent me a piece of American ice. Just as I came out from dinner the Prime Minister asked me what it was. I told him it was ice, or nam now nuck, not knowing any other name for it. I gave him a piece in his hand. He said it was ron nuck, because it stung his hand. I said, "Plan now nuck"—it was cold, so I put a piece in a glass of water. After shaking it quite some time, I gave it to him to drink. Then he found it was cold, and said it was dee nuck, and wanted a piece to take home with him. That was the first ice he had seen.

This brings me to another matter, different from the above. One evening I was preparing to go out to dinner, when two of my lighter men came to my room and informed me my men and Pekenpack's men were fighting. To explain: My men belonged to the clan of Hoinan-Chinamen, while the others came from the Canton district, and spoke a different dialect from that spoken by the Hoinan, the Tea a Choo; so, when the cause is given, no matter how trivial, they come to blows, something like the Corkonians and Fardowns in Ireland. I hastened down the river to the lighter. There I saw a bloody fight between the two factions. One man had his head cut open with an ax. I took in the state of things and concluded there would be more killed. I said to Mr. Pekenpack, "Why did you not stop this fight in the beginning instead of sending for me." He said he was afraid to interfere. With that I took off my coat and picked up a piece of Sappan wood, and watched for a lull, and in I went between the contending parties. I struck out right and left. I drove my men on board of their lighter, and Pekenpack's men into their houses. On the way, I made them pick up the dead man and carry him into his house. By this time the King's police came on the scene, and wanted to arrest my men for killing the man. I stopped them by telling the officer to come tomorrow morning and I would give them the man that did the deed. After all was made quiet, I learned the cause, namely, the cook of my lighter was splitting some wood on the jetty or wharf to cook supper with, and one of Pekenpack's men got a splinter in his foot. Thereupon, he threw the cook, ax and wood into the river. Both sides being very excitable, they came to blows. Next morning I went down to the lighter, and found both parties at work, just as if there had been no difference with them. When they stopped for breakfast I got my men upon deck. I talked to them upon the enormity of the crime that had been committed by one of them, and as I passed by each one, they all looked me in the face and smiled, except one man, who hung his head and looked guilty. I took him by the hand and led him out, and passed him over to the captain of police. He was tried and condemned to have his head cut off. When I heard of it I called on the Prime Minister, and had the case opened. As these men were working for me, they were under American protection, and should have been tried only by American law and before the American Consul. The trial commenced, and I defended my man, and the case closed by giving him nine months with ball and chain, and work when wanted. I sent him from time to such things as he needed for comfort, and he got his pay up to the time of his death, which was in the third or fourth month after conviction.

I am reminded that on a return trip from the bar, I sent the lighters through Paclet Canal. When the men were poling them through, some drunken natives began throwing bricks and stones at the men, and struck several of them. This caused anger, and my men went on shore and chased the others, and they ran into the Governor's yard. There they had a fight, and one of the drunken men was hit so hard that he died in a few days. My men were arrested, and were tried by the Lord Mayor, and fined 7200 Ticols or $4,320.00. I left the matter in the hands of the U. S. Consul. He, not being posted in such matters, and not wanting to offend the Siamese, let matters take their course. When I got back from the outer anchorage, I was informed of the decision of the Court, and of the fine placed upon my men. I went up to the Minister of Foreign Affairs, and insisted on having the case opened up so my men could be heard. He refused. I then told him I should write home to my Government, and lay the case before our Secretary of State, as all I asked was justice, and if it was then decided that my men should pay jet Pan Song Roy Bart, seven thousand two hundred ticols, I would willingly do it, but not till I was satisfied that they had had justice done them.

The case was appointed for Saturday, as that was the only day I could attend in person. After all interested had assembled, the case was called on, and he examined his witnesses. I cross examined them as they came along. I had my interpreter take notes. At first, his Lordship would not let my man put my question, and give their answers. He said one interpreter was enough. I said no, my man was in my place as interpreter, and I proposed using him. When he saw I was determined to have justice, he went on with the case, and I proved by their own side that my men were going along quietly and not disturbing anybody, and they threw bricks and stones at my men, and struck several of them, and made a number of dents and marks on the cabin of the lighter. When my men were called upon to give testimony, his Highness objected; but I insisted that they should be heard in their own defence. I proved by them that they were passing through the Canal, and when they got half way through, several drunken men began to stone them with bricks and stones, to the injury of their persons and property, which was nothing more than the plaintiffs stated in their testimony. My men said they got very angry, and got on shore and ran after the men, and they ran into the Governor's yard, and in the fight, the man got fatally hurt; but could not say by whom, whether by them, or whether he fell and got hurt. Thus, by both sides, I proved that my men were right in protecting my property, a property that was paying into the Siamese treasury thousands upon thousands every month, and why should my property and men be injured by a lot of drunken Siamese? "Why" said I, "your Lordship ought to make these men pay me 5000 ticols for the loss of time of my men and the lighter." At the conclusion of my speech, he said that the widow of the dead man was very poor, with three children, and inasmuch as he had not got the whole case as he now understood it, he would say that my men ought to give the widow two hundred ticols for the loss of her husband. Thereupon I increased it to two hundred and fifty ticols, showing thereby that I wanted to do the right thing. So I sent my interpreter to the steamboat office for the 250 ticols, and paid it then and there. This whole trial shows what a little pluck or cheek will do.

I had many cases of running down boats at night, when the darkness was so intense that a boat could not be seen coming up the river, as they never carry lights. Calling at the U. S. Consulate became so frequent, that I told the Consul that if any native preferred charges against the "Jack Waters" for running him down, for him to pay the damages, not exceeding twenty-five ticols. That wound up the boat business, for as I told him if a boat carried a light, and the "Waters" ran her down, I would pay the damages, but if the boat carried no light, not one cent would I pay.

CHAPTER VI.

AM reminded of a dinner I attended. A high noble invited me to dine with him, which I did, and was met and cordially received by His Highness. In due time, we sat down to dinner, we two with six or eight servants to wait upon us. Course 1, was soup; No. 2, fish; 3, boiled chicken; 4, roast pork, very fat; 5th, grub worms (or looked like them). I, of course, partook of everything I saw him eat. After I had swallowed two or three of the last, I imagined I felt them squirm inside of me, 6th, roast duck; 7th, roast peacock which was very fine; 8th, rice and curry; 9th, fruit of eight or ten different kinds from the Mangosteen and Lichees to the Durian. The

Durian is a fruit very obnoxious to the olfactory organs. The odor can be detected half a mile off, but the pulp inside is perfectly grand, and if a new comer will hold his nose and eat the pulp of one seed, he will untie his nose and eat the pulp of half a dozen seeds. This was my case. I was in the country nearly a year, and the Rev. S. S. Smith, Baptist missionary, invited me to tifhn with him and his good wife. Tiffin consists of roast chicken, fruit, tea and cake. On the table was my inveterate enemy, the Durian. He invited me to partake of it. I declined, but he insisted, saying, "if you don't like it I will never set it before you or ask you to eat it again." I did eat the pulp of one seed, and I found it like a singed cat, far better than it looked; before I moved from the table, I ate the pulp of several seeds. 10th, tea, coffee and cake, and Siamese candy which is very good; 11th, segars, which I enjoyed very much. We separated about 9 P. M., and thus ended the dinner.

This brings to notice a little affair that happened when I was building the large barge and had some two hundred Chinamen and Siamese to work, ship carpenters and joiners, blacksmiths, calkers and laborers. One evening while at dinner, and all the workmen had gone home, there was one man lurking around, and the watchman saw him pick up some small scraps of copper, and he stopped him and reported it to me. I told him Ped de O con kin cow low—wait a little until I eat, then I would see him—which I did. I asked him what he was doing there, and when he had told me I looked at the scraps of copper. They were of no value to me, inasmuch as I had never to the value of a pin lost anything. I made an example of him by taking his tickets from him and tearing them up. These tickets are given in the evening at five, when work stops. They pass in the market the same as cash. At the end of the month all tickets are paid, no matter who brings them in. On some pay days I would have as many as twenty fish and other venders to receive their money for tickets. After I destroyed his tickets (three in all), I told my interpreter to put him out of the gate, which he did. A few days after the watchman went down into the market for some eatables, and the discharged man pulled him and beat him shamefully, cut his face and head. He came to me with the blood on his face, and under the impulse of the moment, my sympathy was enlisted for Chick Heah, the watchman. I called my six boat boys, each with a club, and we started for the market, with me ahead. Just as we entered the market, I saw the man with others enter into a gambling den. We followed and went up to the man, and took him by the arm, and led him out, and fifteen or twenty others followed, yelling and hooting after us as we went on up to our compound. I put the man in the center with three of my boys ahead, and three behind. I took the rear with Chick Heah with me. I then sent him with a bodyguard up to the Lord Mayor with instructions to my interpreter to tell His Excellency what the man had done. Chick Heah went with them with the evidence still on his face. Strange to say, if one man draws blood from another, the injured man never washes the blood off until it is seen by an officer, when the truth of his assertion is established beyond a doubt. His Highness looked at Chick Heah and sent him back to me to do what I thought proper. Next morning the man's wife came to my office and pleaded for her husband on the ground of drunkenness. As I did not have any sympathy for drunkards, I referred the matter to Chick Heah to settle.

The three agreed to abide my decision. Thereupon I decided that the man should pay Chick Song Sip ha Leon $25, to which husband and wife demurred, and offered Song Sip Leon $20 which was accepted. As I knew their propensity for Jewing down, I made it $25 with a view of a cut down. Then the wife wanted the man to go for the money, and she stay until he came back. I said Plow — no — the wife must go and get the money, as I knew the man would never come back, and I could not hold the wife. So she went. In a short time she came back with $20 and handed it to me. I refused it and told her to pay it to the man her husband had nearly killed, which she did, and then they left.

The following Sunday, Chick Heah gave the amount to the poor fund of the little Baptist Church of which he was an honored deacon and a good man, none better in any country, a converted heathen, and proved himself one of the salt of the earth. What man in this country would do the same thing—put money in the treasury of the Lord, that which he received for being cut and slashed to pieces?

The little Baptist church consisted of thirty-one converted heathens, and I tell you of a truth they were all consistent Christians, mainly fishermen. They would come from different points of the surrounding country on Communion Sunday, every two months, and such a meeting! The Rev. R. Telford, Missionary, presided over the church of which he was very proud. I have seen thirty-one ticols or $18.60 put in the poor box for the poor of the church, and other needy Chinamen. A ticol looks as big as a grape shot in the eyes of a poor Chinaman, and fish is their principal diet. Notwithstanding they use light diet, they are very strong. Only think, a man of about 130 lbs. or 140 lbs. will carry piculs of rice 133 lbs. on his shoulder in turn with others, for two and three hours, until they discharge 12 or 1500 piculs of rice out of the lighter up on board of the ship, sometimes in a rough sea when they can hardly keep their feet.

CHAPTER VII.

Y understanding of the trouble between France and Siam is that it is owing principally to France's grasping disposition to overpower the small independent kingdoms in the East.

I think it was about 1860 the French made a demand on the King of Siam for a certain piece of territory over in Anam, in fulfillment of an agreement made by one of the sons of the old king of Anam. This young Prince, after the death of his father, agreed to give the French the territory named if the French would put him on the throne in place of his brother, who was the legitimate heir. The work was consummated; and then the new King told the French that the King of

Siam must consent to his giving the land as it was tributary to Siam. Then the French took up the cudgel of might against right, and began to intimidate the King of Siam, by bringing one of their gun boats up the River with flags flying and drums beating. The ship passed Packnam, which is a custom house, with their guns and cannon on board, which was a violation of the treaty obligations made with Western nations. Up the River came the gun boat with Count Castlenau on board. The demand was then made with all the bombast that a Frenchman can command, and it was refused. The King referred the matter to the Kalaholm, Prime Minister. He gave Count Castlenau an audience. After listening to the Count's demand, the Kalaholm asked "By what authority do you come here to treat with Siam for land? Where is your exequatur to act?" The Count said he had none. "Well," said his Excellency, "you had better go home and ask your Royal Master to give you some authority to act, and not come here with your gun boat and guns past Packnam in violation of treaty which says all guns shall be sent on shore, when a vessel is bound up the River."

The fortification of Packnam consists of only one fort on right hand side of the river as you go up. This fort was built more for appearance than anything else. An American 6-inch gun would knock spots out of it. The river at its mouth is very wide at high water, and about a half mile wide at low water. The channel is very narrow, with two sunken junks on either side. They were sunk there, loaded with stone, to keep the Burmese from entering the river. Bangkok, the capital of the Kingdom, is situated about 25 miles up, and, in my opinion, a very beautiful city as compared with other oriental cities. The people are very friendly, and, for aught I know, strictly honest and straightforward in their dealings with foreigners, except in a few instances, such as I have named—the wood dealer is one.

July 4, 1861.—Four or five of us Americans got up a Fourth of July celebration, consisting of a grand dinner, the best edibles that Singapore and Bangkok could give us. The table was set for 65 guests, in which there were Siamese nobles, Chinese of high grade. We sat at table and enjoyed the dinner, while a Siamese band gave us the best music they could, which means the fellow who can make the biggest noise is the best musician. After the cloth was removed toasts were given and drunk in water-champagne. The King of of Siam was represented by the Lord Mayor; the President of the United States by the writer; the Queen of England by Her Majesty's Consul. Everything went off just as we intended it should. We began the day by firing a national salute with the largest firecrackers we could get; and I tell you we made the welkin ring, for the crackers made a noise like small cannons. We fired 41 guns to salute our flag, 21 to salute the Siamese flag, and kept firing at intervals all day saluting everybody's flag. Thus the day, evening and night passed off very grandly with lots of fun. The natives enjoyed it as much as we did. We closed the grand fandango about 2 A. M. on the 5th, by S. P. Goodale proposing a toast to the writer, to which we responded with good cheer, although very tired. It took nearly all next day to clear up the debris and get in the flags, for we borrowed all the flags from the American ships at the outer anchorage, and all the captains came up to the dinner and had a good time.

Before leaving for home, the King sent his messenger, a noble, for me on Sunday morning, requesting an audience. I told the messenger that inasmuch as Sunday was a day of rest, and I had been in his country nearly five years, and had not violated one of my Christian principles, and as I was about taking my leave of Siam, I did not wish to violate or trespass upon

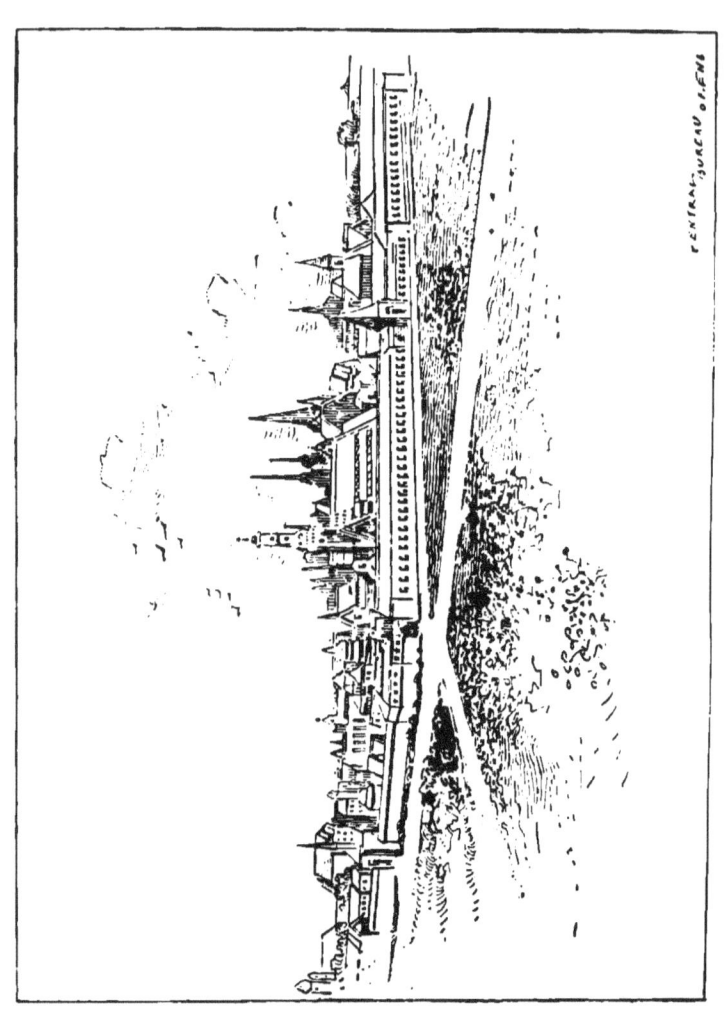

KING'S PALACE, BANGKOK, SIAM. (Page 87.)

the good examples I had tried to inculcate in the minds of his subjects; but added in my note that I would meet His Majesty at 10 next morning. He answered by note, saying my time was too early in the morning, but would meet me at 2 in the afternoon. When it was time to start for the Palace, I called away my gig (boat) and took with me the Rev. S. Matoon and Rev. R. Telford. When we arrived at the Palace we were conducted to the reception apartment, in front of which there were two elephants with all their fixings on, and also about 50 soldiers drawn up in line. Music was furnished by the King's brass band, with a French leader, who played "Star Spangled Banner," "Yankee Doodle," etc. Finally, the King came out and bid us welcome, and talked of many things pertaining to my stay in his Kingdom, and of the many regrets expressed by his brother, Prince Crom Alouing Wang-Sau, the Prime Minister, and other nobles, and closed the interview by requesting me to send him, at his expense, two boxes of American tobacco called Honey Dew. During the interview or audience, the King took off and put on his finger a magnificent ring. I began to think he intended to present it to me as a souvenir of his best wishes, but he did not.

He took this occasion to invite us to the crowning ceremony of his eldest son and heir to the throne of Siam, but as he had learned from Ma Millee that he did not participate in anything on One Ah Tit (Sunday), and Sunday would be the first day, he hoped we would all come on the other two days. We thanked His Majesty, and made our salaam, and were escorted to our boat, and left for home. On the day appointed we went to the crowning, and were given the best seats at the show and feast. The crowning of an oriental prince was something grand. To me it was a grand sight; in fact, it was to all of us who came from the far off western nation. The second day, the young prince was arrayed in gor-

YOUNG PRINCE, NOW KING OF SIAM.   (Page 89.)

geous apparel, and carried on a very handsome
sedan chair by four native noblemen, with two
nobles to steady him, as the gold decorations on
the young man would certainly weigh twenty
pounds. They were interwoven with diamonds
and other precious stones. The procession stopped in front of the writer, so I got a good look
at the young prince as he was taken down from
the sedan chair and was conducted into the temporary throne room where he was divested of
his gorgeous apparel. Then he was taken up
winding stairs to the top of a very high artificial
mountain built of bamboo, and covered with
green paper, and having miniature trees up the
sides and on top. The whole thing was worthy
of the occasion. The writer was very much
pleased with all he saw. After the ceremony we
were conducted to the banqueting hall, and sat
down to a bountiful feast, gotten up in true American and English style, with beer, wine and other
liquors for those who drank. The whole thing

passed off in a manner worthy of an oriental King. The then young prince is now the reigning monarch of that Kingdom.

On my arrival in New York I called on John Anderson & Co., 114 Liberty street, who very readily said they would put up a dozen boxes or six gross of tobacco into very handsome boxes, and forward them free of charge, for the privilege of of advertising the order received from the King of Siam. I dictated the order to his agent, which made about one-fifth of a column in the daily papers. The tobacco was put up in grand style. First it was put into very handsome paper boxes, then into a perfectly beautiful mahogany case, with this inscription in gold letters: "For the first King of Siam and Sovereign of Laos." This case was on exhibition for some time. Then it was put into a strong pine box and shipped to Bangkok via Hong Kong, care Messrs. A. A. Low Bros., Chinese merchants; from Hong Kong Bangkok, care of the Rev. S. Matoon, of Presbyterian mission, and forwarded by him to the Palace. The King received the shipment and expressed his thanks.

Last, but not least, the steamer "Viscount Canning" arrived, and I got all ready for my departure for Hong Kong and home. Some of my friends waited upon C. G. Allen to charter the "Jack Waters" to take me down to the bar. He declined, saying he had made all arrangements to take me down at his own expense, which he did in noble style.

CHAPTER VIII.

WE started from Bangkok about 9 o'clock on the 13th of March, 1862, and arrived alongside of the steamer about 1 o'clock. Captain Ah Choon was up to all good things, for he had the cabin table spread with a grand collation, which we all enjoyed.

After doing full justice to the good things which Captain Ah Choon had provided, the cloth was removed. S. P. Goodale, the United States Consul, rose in his seat and proposed the name of *our guest* (the writer), to which Mr. C. G. Allen responded, eulogizing the writer in the highest degree. Then there were several other speeches from the Portugese, ex-American, Russian, British and the Hamburgh Consuls. All spoke in about the same strain, by crediting me for more than I thought I deserved. At the conclusion of S. P. Goodale's remarks, a boy handed him two bags containing about 600 Mexican dollars. This amount he said was contributed by my friends in Bangkok for the purpose of purchasing a set of silver, and to be kept to remind me of the friends I left behind me in Bangkok, and also to refresh my memory of the many happy days I passed with them during my four and a half years residence in that city. He said my friends were legion; he did not know of a man, woman or child but what respected me for my manhood and Christian character, from the King down to the Cooley population. In fact, I think he eulogized me too highly to my face. If I had been dead, then he could say what he pleased. At the close of his remarks he presented me with the two bags of treasure. After considerable talking, laughing and crying, the entire escort returned to the "Jack Waters," and cast off their lines and started for Bangkok, and left me alone with my own feelings, for I certainly did feel bad at parting with so many staunch friends. I watched the receding "Jack Waters" until she passed around Mud Point and entered the river. My mind began to run over my past four and a half years with the natives, and I saw nothing in my career amongst them but what was of the most friendly character; and I will say the Siamese are today a kind, generous people. I traveled through a large part of their country, and met with nothing but kindness. In some places where we passed, the natives, who never saw a white man, and to whom we looked strange and ate strangely with knife, fork and spoon, would observe us very closely and watch how we handled the tools. Why should I not feel sad at leaving so many people, native and foreign, whom I loved?

The captain went back to the city with the steamer.

14th.—The captain came on board and ordered steam up, and the anchor hove short. At 9 A. M. we started, everybody bustling about, getting the ship ready for sea. We passed Cape Liant out into the open Gulf of Siam. Farewell to Siam! I came to you with my forebodings four years, six months and fifteen days ago! I now go away with many heartfelt feelings of respect. May God grant that the day is not far distant when you may all see the beauties of the religion of Jesus Christ, and turn from your idol worship to the one living and true God!

19th.—Passed Pulo Cordore, 12 miles distant; wind N.E. by E., with very bad coal.

20th.—Kept off two points to let the sails draw.

21st:—Fresh breeze, with heavy sea running. Sighted the Island of Pulo de Moore—large island, inhabited by a very industrious class of Cochin Chinese. 4 P. M.—Every prospect of a very dirty night.

22d.—Heavy sea running. Ship heading N.E. by E. Heavy weather, with rain. No sun to-day. 5 P. M.—Put the ship on the port tack, and stood in for the Gulf of Tonquin. On account of bad coal could not make steam.

23d.—Doing well for us—about 6 knots; ship heading E.N.E.

24th.—No wind, with long rolling sea. Kept close up to the Parasels Shoals in 4½ fathoms. Lat., 14 N. Ship rolling like a log. No steam. With such weather the ship, with good coal, could make 12 knots. This is all on the Owen Pher Py San. This is the Northeast Mantzoon season, and we may expect a snorter from N.E. at any time. If we do get it, good bye, John, for we will hand in the number of our mess. Lat. 15–40.

26th, 6 A. M.—Stopped the engines to clean tubes and back bridges all right. Lat., 17 N.; long., 113 E.

27th.—All right, making 7 knots. Wind N.

half E. Stopped two hours to get clear of the land.

28th, 6 A. M.—We made the Leana Island. Weather thick and hazy, and to me very cold. Quite a number of fishing junks outside fishing with their long seines, end of which are made fast to two junks, and they sail about 150 feet, dragging the seine with them. After a certain time, they come in and take the fish out of the net. About 9 o'clock passed the Ass's Ears, and came to in the harbor of Hong Kong, after a very tedious passage of 14 days.

Hong Kong is an English colony under British rule, and is a very fine city, built on the side of a hill, very high, the top of which is called Victoria Peak, which has a marine telegraph station. There are some very fine granite buildings belonging to the English and Americans and other foreign merchants, Russell & Co., Augustine Heard & Co., Oliphant & Co., Thomas Hunt & Co. It is a very lively city. At this writing, there are say fifty sail of ships of various nationalities at anchor.

29th.—I took a sail up to Wampoo and Canton on the American steamer, White Cloud. Wampoo is a place for mechanical work. There are three very fine dry docks, and a machine shop. The ship N. B. Palmer, belonging to A. A. Low & Bros., of New York, I went on board of, and engaged passage and state room for New York, $400. Everybody is getting rich.

30th.—The City of Canton is a walled city of about 5,000,000 population including the white population; about 1,500,000 live on the water. I saw about one-eighth of the city and I was in the great Confucius temple of five hundred gods. I went inside of the wall and met nothing but friendship and kindness from the Cantonese. I was carried in a sedan chair by two coolies up on top of a high hill where

I could see all over the city, all a bustle, everybody busy. Streets very narrow, about nine feet from curb to curb, principal business tea and silk, no loafers or idle men or women.

31st.—I again started for Hong Kong on the White Cloud. The Canton river is beautiful, having clusters of islands, and the banks of the river presented high mountains, very picturesque.

APRIL 1st.—Nothing but going about.

3d.—Breakfasted with Capt. Treadwell on board of the American clipper ship, Sagamore.

4th.—Breakfasted with Capt. Rowe on the American Barque, Homer, and dined on board the British Barque, Alicia, Capt. Morse. Between the 5th and 10th I did as I pleased, visiting the various Chinese shops, and buying trinkets, silk for dresses, and getting my wardrobe, such as all kinds of linen, etc., ready for a long voyage. I went to dinner on board of the American ship, Golconda, Capt. ——

I have forgotten his name, and I ought to know it for I had business with him afterwards. The "Golconda" had two large painted eyes round her horse pipes. The only way I could make my Sanpan man, Boston Jack, understand what ship I wanted to go to—I said "Jack, you savy that piece of Melican ship have got eye?" He answered, "I savy plenty." Then I asked, "Jack, why that ship have got eye?" He asked, "You no savy?" I said no; then he said, "No got eye, no can see; no can see, no can savy. How can?" That is to say, if a ship has no eyes, it can't see where to go.

14th.—I sent my baggage on board of the Palmer, consisting of 14 packages. I am just tired out walking, and being carried about in a sedan chair, and feasting, as my friendly captains of many American clipper ships insist on my breakfasting and dining with them, so that I ate only a few meals at my hotel, the Oriental up on the hill, a very fine American Hotel kept by Theo. Andrews & Company.

19th.—I paid my bill, and left for the ship. After passing the night with my friend Capt. Treadwell of the American ship, Sagamore, here I am on board of the Palmer, and the Chinese pilot in command, who ordered the anchor hove short, and loose the topsails. We were lying nearly inside of all the ships, the pilot backed the fore topsail to give the ship stearnway, and backed the ship out through the other ships with her head pointed outward.

CHAPTER IX.

APRIL 20th.—Sunday, all right. Ship doing well, and better than we ought to expect at this season of the year. Just on the change of Montzoon from N. E. to S. W. which makes it hard for ships bound down the sea, and good for those bound up.

21st.—All right, while everything set from mainsail to skysail. The ship is in first rate trim, and everybody happy, from Capt. Chas. P. Low and lady, Mrs. Parker and two children, of Mass., Rev. Mr. Talmadge and four children, of New Jersey, Mr. E. E. Webber of Mass., T. Barnard of Mass., and Thos. Miller of New York. The Rev. Mr. Talmadge is returning with his children after laying his wife away in her grave. S.S.W. 130 miles.

22nd.—The ship going along steady as a pump bolt, 130 miles S.W. x W.

23d.—And all's well; ship off course two points. 12 M. tacked ship and stood off 138 miles. 68 miles on her course due south.

24th.—6 A. M., beautiful morning, and good breeze; the ship off two points on the port tack S.W x S. Made the Island of Pulo Con, a small island to the south of the mainland of Cochin China. Tacked ship and stood off to clear the Island. 5 P. M., tacked ship on the port tack; passed the Island on the starboard beam. 9 P. M., tacked ship and stood out to sea. 49 miles due south.

25th.—Wind dead ahead. 65 miles on our course.

26th.—Wind still dead ahead. 35 miles on course.

27th.—Sunday. All is well. Wind ahead. Very dull day on shipboard. No work but working ship. We have 35 Lascar sailors, all Mahometans, headed by a Surang, who is a high man in their religious faith. He is looked up to by the sailors. They have held their worship on shipboard. 49 miles.

28th.—Doing very well. 35 miles.

29th.—All is well, and now having the first fair wind. 9½ knots. Wind very light, with studding sails. 134 miles.

30th.—All is well. Fair wind, very light. 150 miles.

MAY 1st.—Beautiful morning for the first of May. Opposite the Gulf of Siam. 140 miles.

2d.—Here we are, down among the Midorus Islands—a group of islands governed by a Rajah; a very fine hospitable man.

3d.—Very calm; nothing doing.

4th.—Lat., 1-15 N. In full view of a large group of islands called Saddle, Campbell and Meguan Islands.

5th.—My birthday; 40 years old today. We landed a boat, and the first mate, Mr. Joseph Steel,

Mr. Webber, Barnard and Miller went ashore. As I thought I ought to have some excitement on my birthday, so I went ashore on Campbell Island. The island is about two miles long, half mile wide, shaped like a camel's back; desert island. Did nothing today.

6th.—Very calm, to almost suffocation. Thermometer 91. We saw steamer astern, coming down the sea with a vessel in tow. 9 P. M.—She is off our starboard beam.

7th.—The steamer we saw last night is far astern of us. We had a little breeze during the night, and sailed away ahead of the steamer. No wind, and the steamer is passing on one side of the island of St. Barba and we on the other.

8th.—No wind, with lots of islands in sight.

9th.—No wind. Ten squalls in the morning; very calm in the afternoon.

11th.—We are now in the Java Sea. We passed through the Straits of Jasper last night. Lat., 4-20 S.

12th.—Still calm.

13th.—Very calm, with the Islands of the Brothers and the North Watchers in sight. 3 P. M.—Squally, with rain. Passed the North Watchers, with two of the One Thousand Islands in sight.

14th.—Here we are at anchor in the Harbor of Anjier in the Straits of Sunda, 26 days from Hong Kong. We went on shore on the Island of Java, saw the harbor master, and then took a stroll over the town, which I found very much improved since I was there in 1857. We went out to the coffee plantations and saw the natives. Lat., 6-20 S. Coffee is hulled with a concave and convex roller. The coffee is put in the concave roller and the convex one crushes the hull off, after which it is winnowed by hand in the old primitive way, with shallow baskets or trays.

15th.—Still at anchor, and getting fresh water and provisions. The captain and I went on shore here. Let me say that all the islands are of coral formation. I have some fine specimens.

16th.—We again got under way about 11 o'clock last night, and stood out of the straits between Java and Sumatra. Wind hauling ahead, and caused us to pass between the Islands of Cockatoo and Princess.

17th.—Java head still in sight. Very little breeze from S.S.E. Lat., 6-48 : long., 104 E. 60 miles.

18th.—All right. Light winds and squalls. Lat., 8-55; long., 102 E. 58 miles.

19th.—All right. Good breeze. 30 days out from Hong Kong. Distance 206 miles from Java.

20th.—All is well. Lat., 10-10; long., 98-54.

21st.—Lat., 11-35; long., 96 E. 190 miles.

22d.—Lat., 12-32; long., 94-17 E. Distance 130 miles.

23d.—Lat., 13-48; long., 92-51 E. Distance 138 miles.

24th.—Lat., 15-04; long., 89-40 E. Distance 161 miles.

25th.—Grand breeze, and Mr. Talmadge gave us a talk from Hebrews, iii., 16. Lat., 16-4; long., 84-45. 188 miles.

26th.—Good heavy breeze. This is the first day we had to take any sail off on account of wind. Lat., 17-34; long., 82-08. 282 miles.

27th.—This is a grand day for the ship. All are happy but me. I have a fearful heartburn caused by doing a big lot of nothing, with heaviness over the eyes. Lat., 19: long. 77-44. 288 miles.

28th.—We are doing well, and I feel better, thanks to a good dose of medicine. Lat., 20-10; long., 74-14. 214 miles.

29th.—Breeze continues, and I feel better to-day. Lat., 21-05; Long., 70-35. 200 miles.

30th.—Good breeze, and I feel better than I have for some days. Lat., 21-37; long., 67-35. 182 miles.

31st.—Six weeks out to-day. Almost calm. Lat., 22–30; long., 65–47. 125 miles from first Sunday, and very calm. 3 P. M.—Squally, with rain. Mr. Talmadge gave us a talk from Ephesians. 43 days out. Lat., 22–23; long., 64–24. 80 miles.

JUNE 2d.—All well. Bitter wind. Occupied my time overhauling my trunk. Lat., 22–51; long., 61–46 W. by W. half N. 150 miles. 4 days.

3d.—Nearly calm. Lat., 23–12; long., 59–51. 70 miles. 45 days out.

4th.—Wind unsteady. My boy's birthday; 6 years old. Lat., 23–41; long., 57–51. 70 miles. 46 days.

5th.—Wind light. Sent down skysail yards. Lat., 24–11; long., 56–48. 72 miles. 47 days out.

6th.—All right. Lat., 24–48; long., 55–14. 94 miles. 48 days.

7th.—Doing well. Lat., 24–03; long., 53–14. 119 miles. 49 days.

8th.—And a fair prospect of a good breeze.

Preaching by Mr. Talmadge, from Deuteronomy, 9th chapter. Lat., 25-33; long., 51-26. 114 miles. 50 days.

9th.—Strong breeze all night, with heavy thunder and sharp lightning. 12 M.—The ship was under close-reefed topsails. Lat., 26-46; long., 48-44. 164 miles. 51 days.

10th.—All well, but no wind. Lat., 26-45; long., 47-30. 65 miles. 52 days.

11th.—Very calm. Lat., 27-40; long., 46-50. 68 miles. 53 days.

12th.—Lat., 27-40; long., 45-16. 80 miles. 54 days.

13th.—Heavy wind from N.W. Ship under every sail. Heavy sea running. Lat., 28-06; long., 44-15. 68 miles. 55 days.

14th.—Eight weeks out today. Wind moderate. Lat., 27-40; long., 43-33. 54 miles. 56 days.

15th.—Lat., 27-13; long., 41-59. 88 miles. 57 days.

16th.—Lat., 27-29; long., 40-46. 68 miles. 58 days.

17th.—Lat., 28-34; long., 39-05. Strong breeze from N.W.

18th.—Heavy gale from N.W. Ship under every canvas. Lat., 29-41; long., 36-02. 170 miles.

19th.—Heavy gale from S.W. Laid to under close-reefed topsail and fore skysail. Heavy sea. Water flying like snowdrifts. Lat., 29-24; long., 34-42. 70 miles.

21st.—Lat., 31-47; long., 30-50. 220 miles. Doing well. Saw a large Dutch ship, deep loaded, from Batavia, homeward bound.

22d.—Strong gale from W.S.W. Lat., 32-51; long., 29-02. 112 miles.

23d.—Lat., 33-30; long., 29-09. Leeway 29 miles. Gale continues from W.S.W. Everything snug, and ship riding like a duck, and we have lost our Dutch friend astern out of sight.

24th.—Lat., 33-12; long., 28-52. Land in sight starboard bow. Weather fair. 210 miles.

25th.—Lat., 34-45; long., 25-11. Saw three ships. 120 miles.

26th.—Lat., 34-47; long., 23-118. 67 days. Head wind. Close-reefed topsails.

27th.—Lat., 35-06; long., 22-89. Blowing a snorter from W.S.W.

28th.—Lat., 35-16; long., 22-07. Head wind. Ship under easy sail. Two ships in sight.

29th.—Lat., 35-31; long., 20-56. Four ships in sight. Spoke the British barque "Wellington," 83 days from Bombay, bound to Liverpool.

30th.—Lat., 25-34; long., 20-50. Heavy gale, with close-reefed main topsail.

July 1st.—Lat., 34-35; long., 20-40. With the Table Lands in the east coast of Africa in sight. Distance about 20 miles.

2d.—Lat., 34-51; long., 20-24. All becalmed on the Lagulis Banks. All hands fishing; caught

1,200 pounds of beneta, long fish, some which weighed 25 lbs.

3d.—Lat., 35-34; long., 19-28. Sighted nine ships. Cape Lagulis light in sight.

4th.—Lat., 35-07; long., 19-12. Two brigs in sight. Heavy gale; laid to; wind north.

5th.—Lat., 34-13; long., 17-48. Gale still piping.

6th.—Lat., 33-39; long., 17-38. Saw large British ship, 87 days out from Akyah, bound to London.

7th.—Lat., 33-13; long., 17-28.

8th.—Lat., 33-13; long., 17-28. Nothing of interest to-day.

9th.—Lat., 33-13; long., 17-28.

10th.—Lat., 32-54; long., 16-23.

11th.—Lat., 31-05; long., 16-17.

12th.—Lat., 30-23; long., 16-03.

13th.—Lat., 29-44; long., 14-50.

14th.—Lat., 29-03; long., 13-50.

15th.—Lat., 28-10; long., 13.

16th.—Lat., 26-19; long., 10-27. 175 miles; the first day of the S.E. trades. 89 days out.

17th.—Lat., 24-12; long., 6-18. 264 miles.

18th.—Lat., 22-9; long., 3-9. 216 miles. 91 days.

19th.—Lat. 19-45; long., 41 W. 265 miles.

20th.—Lat., 17-43; long., 3-47. 220 miles.

21st.—Lat., 15-55; long., 5-30. 150 miles. 94 days.

ISLAND OF ST. HELENA. (Page 115.)

CHAPTER X.

JULY 22d.—Sighted the Island of St. Helena at daylight, and about 8 A. M. came to anchor in roadstead. The island is nothing but a large lonely island in mid ocean. Jamestown is an English garrison, settled by soldiers and their families and others. Some are tradespeople, who came to the island to make money out of the soldiers and natives. The natives, by the way, are a very small race of people, and talk half English, half Indian. They have a very yellow cast of countenance, more of the Malay color. After getting water and some fresh provisions on board, a number of us went on shore and hired two carriages, and we all started up a very rough mountain road for Long Wood, the home of the great Napoleon. We passed through all the rooms of the house, even into the room where Napoleon died. There is an iron fence built round the spot where the bed stood. Everything is in a good state of preservation, and is kept by Frenchmen, as it is the property of the French by purchase. There is a fish pond near the house. The house and surroundings are on the top of the highest mountain, a bleak sort of a place, with guns of large size set with their muzzles pointing seaward. All this ado to keep one man a prisoner on a lonely island in mid ocean! We saw the house called Brier where they put him at first on landing on the island, and we saw the grave where he was buried, down in a lonely valley between two high hills, with a lonely little weeping willow tree at the head of the grave. The tree was dead, and not more than six inches in diameter and fifteen feet high. Just such a place as a man of his great brain would have selected for a resting place. Here let me say that there have been more sprigs of willow brought to this and other countries by sailors than would make a tree three feet in diameter. All his surroundings tell of the isolated life of the great French chieftain. I entered my name in the visitors' register on the very table where he amused himself playing a game called " Solitaire." We left Long Wood for Jamestown, and, after looking over the place, saw, in many places, terrible devastation to buildings caused by the white ant. On inquiring I found that a vessel came in and landed a load of African pine and other wood, in which were white ants. The white ant is very destructive to some kinds of wood. So much for Jamestown and the Island of St. Helena. We again boarded our good ship " N. B. Palmer," and sailed about 8 P. M. Lat., 16-03; long., 7-06.

 23d.—Lat., 14-02; long., 10-20. 198 miles.
 24th.—Lat., 12-19; long., 12-14. 160 miles.
 25th.—Lat., 11-06; long., 14-16. 140 miles.
 26th.—Lat., 9-56; long., 16-33. 152 miles.

27th.—Lat., 8-46; long., 19-33. 196 miles. 100 days out from Hong Kong.

28th.—Lat., 7-28; long., 22-02. 174 miles.

29th.—Lat., 5-54; long., 24-37. 180 miles.

30th.—Lat., 4-01; long., 27-18. 190 miles.

31st.—Lat., 1-36; long., 29-40. 200 miles.

August 1st.—Lat., 1-49 N.; long,, 32-14 W. 235 miles.

2d.—Lat., 3-45; long., 35-05.

3d.—Lat., 4-55; long., 36-40. 105 miles.

4th.—Lat., 6-47; long., 37-10. 100 miles, and I am five years away from home to-day.

5th.—Lat., 9-25; long., 38-20. 170 miles.

6th.—Lat., 11; long., 40-02. 140 miles.

7th.—Lat., 12-42; long., 40-42. 160 miles.

8th.—Lat., 13-10; long., 42-36. 140 miles.

9th.—Lat., 14-22; long., 45-26. 180 miles.

10th.—Lat., 15-02; long., 48-1. 160 miles.

11th.—Lat., 15-36; long., 49-08. 62 miles.

12th.—Lat., 16-07; long; 49-15. 35 miles.

13th.—Lat., 16-49; long., 50-15. 72 miles.

14th.—Lat., 18-30; long., 52-39. 170 miles. Boarded the British barque " S. Hardy," from Cork, Ireland, bound to Barbadoes. I got a barrel of beef.

15th.—Lat., 19-46; long., 55-40. 185 miles.
16th.—Lat., 21-34; long., 57-40. 160 miles.
17th.—Lat., 23-56; long., 60-52. 228 miles.
18th.—Lát., 26-12; long., 63-30. 200 miles.
19th.—Lat., 27 58; long., 65-59. 170 miles.
20th.—Lat., 29-58; long., 67-51. 160 miles.
21st.—Lat., 31-20; long., 68-46. 96 miles.
22d.—Lat., 32-38; long., 69-42. 92 miles.
23d.—Lat., 33-55; long., 70-07. 84 miles.
24th.—Lat., 35-12; long., 71-26. 104 miles. 2 P. M.—Entered the Gulf. 11 P. M.—Brought the ship down to topsails. Ship in sight, bound south.

25th.—Lat., 37-55; long., 73-38. 190 miles.
26th.—Lat., 40; long., 74. 100 miles. 130 days from Hong Kong. 3 P. M.—Took pilot from Boat No. 13. Came to anchor off the bar, wait-

ing for high tide. Everybody very happy at seeing our native land, after an absence of many years, some longer than others. Next morning took a tow boat from the bar up to the City of New York, and docked the ship. Then I went ashore, and did some business, and started for

>Home, sweet home,
>Be it ever so humble,
>There's no place like home!

www.ingramcontent.com/pod-product-compliance
Lightning Source LLC
Chambersburg PA
CBHW020059170426
43199CB00009B/334